A DAY THAT MADE HISTORY

THE JULY PLOT

Nigel Richardson

Dryad Press Limited   London

Contents

Acknowledgments

The author and publishers thank the following for their kind permission to reproduce copyright illustrations: Barnaby's Picture Library, pages 10, 38 (top); Bundesarchiv, pages 14, 18, 22, 24, 28, 35, 40, 42, 44, 49; Robert Hunt Library, cover, pages 9 (top), 12, 21; Novosti, page 46; The Photo Source, pages 5, 7, 36, 37, 43, 45, 51, 54, 55, 56, 61; Popperfoto, page 31; Süddeutscher Verlag, page 38 (bottom); US National Archives, page 9 (bottom); Weidenfeld and Nicolson Ltd, page 34. The maps and plans on pages 10, 13 and 41 are by R.F. Brien. The pictures were researched by David Pratt.

The "Day that Made History" series was devised by Nathaniel Harris.

© Nigel Richardson 1986. First published 1986.
Typeset by Tek-Art Ltd, Kent, and printed in Great Britain by R.J. Acford, Chichester for the publishers, Dryad Press Limited, 4 Fitzhardinge Street, London W1H 0AH

ISBN 0 8521 9672 5

THE
EVENTS

Rastenburg: 12.42 p.m., 20th July, 1944

On 20th July, 1944 Adolf Hitler, dictator of Germany for eleven years, held the usual daily military conference at his headquarters at Rastenburg. This collection of wooden huts and concrete bunkers hidden in a forest in Eastern Germany had been his home for most of the previous three years; it was one of the most isolated parts of his huge empire.

The war, which three years earlier had been going so well for him, had now reached a desperate stage. German forces were retreating westwards out of Russia. Six weeks earlier, the Allies – Britain and America – had entered Rome on their way northwards from North Africa. In the same week other troops had swarmed across the Channel into France on D-Day. Allied planes were bombing German cities night after night.

It is not surprising that Hitler's advisers were gloomy. Rastenburg was a depressing place after the glamour of Berlin. But Hitler did not seem to notice; he was content to live there in two or three drab rooms with concrete walls lined by only a few pieces of simple, wooden furniture. His whole day would be taken up with meals followed by meetings. Occasionally he would take his Alsatian bitch, Blondi, for a walk, but he no longer had any other forms of relaxation – films, or gramophone records in the evenings after dinner were things of the past. Now he merely brooded about his past life. He saw few of his old friends, preferring to eat only with his secretaries. They were forbidden to mention the war.

At the daily conference Hitler's officers would give him the latest military reports. Maps and diagrams would be spread out on a huge table. Hitler would make decisions, and the officers would hurry away to instruct their troops. If air raids seemed likely, the conference would be held underground, but 20th July was a hot summer day, and the meeting took place in the conference barracks, a wooden building recently reinforced with concrete 45 centimetres thick for protection against aircraft bombing. The main room was about 10 metres long and 5 wide. It had ten windows, all of them open to catch the breeze.

By about 12.30 p.m. twenty-four people were gathered around an oblong table, 5 metres by 1½, which stood on two huge supports, one near each end. Hitler was seated at the centre of one of the long sides, his back to the door. On his right stood General Heusinger, General Korten and Colonel Brandt; on his left, General Jodl. Hitler was poring over the maps with the magnifying glass which he now needed to read small print.

Heusinger was in the middle of a gloomy report about the Russian front when General Keitel entered with Colonel von Stauffenberg, a one-armed man with a patch over one eye. Hitler glanced up as Keitel announced Stauffenberg's arrival, and said that he wanted to finish with Heusinger's report before Stauffenberg gave his briefing. Stauffenberg quietly told Keitel that he had an urgent 'phone call to make and would be back in a minute. Keitel nodded and moved to the table, immediately to Hitler's left.

Heusinger continued talking. Stauffenberg leaned down and placed his briefcase against the inside of the stout oak support, whispering a word or two to Brandt. He left the room at 12.37 p.m. Concentrating hard on the map, Brandt leaned across to get a closer look; his foot caught Stauffenberg's briefcase. He tried to push it out of the way with his foot, then used his hand to move it to the *outside* of the table support. A piece of heavy oak now stood between the briefcase and Hitler.

Keitel sensed that Heusinger had nearly finished his report. He wondered whether Stauffenberg would need help to get his papers out of his briefcase. But Stauffenberg had not yet returned. Keitel slipped out of the room to find him. Heusinger continued talking. "The Russian is driving with strong forces west of the Duna towards the north. His spearheads are already southwest of Dunaburg. If our army group around Lake Pepius is not immediately withdrawn, a catastrophe . . ."

In the middle of the sentence there was a shattering explosion. It was 12.42 p.m.

Stauffenberg: morning and before

The bomb which shattered the conference room had been hidden in Stauffenberg's briefcase. Claus Philip Schenk, Count von Stauffenberg, was a very exceptional man, and he had been waiting for this chance for over two years. He came from South Germany and was a member of an aristocratic, Roman Catholic family with a tradition of military service stretching back nearly 150 years.

Although he was a sensitive man who loved music and literature and who briefly considered becoming an architect, his family history and his passion for horses made it natural

Claus Graf Schenk von Stauffenberg.

that he should become a soldier. In 1926, aged nineteen, he became an officer cadet in the famous 17th Bamberg Cavalry Regiment. He was soon recognized as a brilliant all-rounder with good looks, a keen sense of humour and an ability to make friends quickly. His nervous energy and physical strength enabled him to work at tremendous speed. One colleague remembered that "his powers of concentration were like steel", and a fellow-plotter wrote later that "his sincerity and . . . courage, combined with his technical knowledge and efficiency, fully qualified him to become director of the Resistance movement. He seemed to have been born for the part."

He had not always been against Hitler. In January 1933 young Lieutenant Stauffenberg led a group of cheering demonstrators celebrating Hitler's appointment as German Chancellor. He was wearing full uniform, and his superiors were not amused – they did not want the Army too closely linked with politics or with individual politicians. But it was only a temporary setback; three years later Stauffenberg was posted to the War Academy in Berlin. In 1938 he graduated with flying colours as a young General Staff officer.

Two events in that year dramatically changed his view of Hitler. Hitler's Nazis carried out a series of attacks on Jews and their property and this sickened him. Secondly, as Hitler began to discuss his plans for conquest abroad more openly, and as German troops marched into Western Czechoslovakia, Stauffenberg realized that Germany was being led into a war in which millions might die and which Germany might eventually lose.

When the war began, however, he supported it energetically, serving first in Poland and then in France. But he did not hesitate to tell four generals in France that Hitler's attitude to power and conquest was irresponsible and dangerous, and even suggested that he deserved to die. For eighteen months after Hitler's invasion of Russia in June 1941, Stauffenberg spent most of his time there working for the Army High Command. Shortly before the capitulation of the German Army at Stalingrad in 1943, he tried unsuccessfully to persuade a group of senior officers that Hitler should be forced to give up his control of the Army there or be put under arrest. Saying such things was very reckless; many army officers were beginning to doubt the wisdom of Hitler's strategy and they heartily disliked Hitler's secret police, the S.S., but S.S. officers and informers were everywhere. Even if he expressed his views only in the privacy of an officers'

Hitler reviewing the S.S. in 1938.

mess, to brother soldiers whom he thought sympathetic, Stauffenberg was still living very dangerously.

It was S.S. brutality in Russia which finally turned Stauffenberg against Hitler. He made links with General von Tresckow and other officers who shared his opinions, but he sensed that senior commanders on the Russian front were too divided amongst themselves and perhaps too cowardly to take decisive action. He would have to bide his time. Sickened by the terrible suffering of German soldiers at Stalingrad, he asked for a transfer in February 1943 and was posted to North Africa.

On 7th April he was severely wounded. Either his car was riddled with bullets by low-flying aircraft or it ran into a minefield; what is certain is that he spent several months in hospital in Munich during which time he became determined

7

to kill Hitler. "I feel I must do something now to save Germany," he told his wife. "We General Staff officers must all accept our share of the responsibility." He lost his left eye, and for several weeks doctors feared that he would be completely blind. His right hand and forearm had gone; two fingers on his other hand were also missing, and there were serious injuries to his left ear and knee.

Within three months he had learned how to write with the remaining fingers of his left hand. He was also practising with that bandaged hand how to set off time bomb fuses. He wrote to General Ölbricht, Chief of Staff and Deputy Commander of the Home (or Reserve) Army in Berlin that he expected to be back on active service within three months. Ölbricht and some fellow generals were already making plans to seize the capital if and when anyone succeeded in killing or overthrowing Hitler. Stauffenberg was soon planning with them.

A whole series of attempts to assassinate Hitler were made by army officers between September 1943 and January 1944, mostly with time bombs, but Hitler seemed to bear a charmed life. One attempt involved Stauffenberg himself. On 26th December he was summoned to the daily Rastenburg conference. He took with him a time bomb in his briefcase. But the meeting was cancelled; Hitler had suddenly decided to spend Christmas elsewhere.

The D-Day landings convinced the plotters that they must act quickly. The war was now clearly lost. The Russians would probably overrun Germany. Hitler would never agree to surrender. Perhaps Britain and America could be persuaded to negotiate with a non-Nazi government? At this point the plotters had a stroke of luck. Stauffenberg was promoted to full Colonel and appointed Chief of Staff to General Fromm, the Commander-in-Chief of the Home Army. This would mean regularly going to Hitler's war conferences.

The plotters were now hoping to kill Hitler and two other Nazi leaders, Göring and Himmler, all at once. Stauffenberg went to meet Hitler at Obersalzburg on 11th July with another briefcase bomb, but this attempt was called off when Himmler stayed away. Four days later Stauffenberg set off again for Rastenburg with his briefcase bulging. He made his report to Hitler, but came out to telephone his fellow-plotters in Berlin to tell them to start to move their troops. When he got back to the conference Hitler had left, and plans in Berlin had to be hurriedly cancelled before the S.S. heard about them.

S.S. Reich leader Heinrich Himmler visits the concentration camp at Dachau in 1936. As leader of the S.S. he was responsible for the extermination of millions of Jews and other opponents of Hitler – although he could never himself watch the suffering he caused.

After the attempt on Hitler's life at Rastenburg the Reich Security Head Office conducted a detailed investigation. They collected the remains of Stauffenberg's briefcase (in which the bomb was hidden), and the fuse, shown here. They also discovered a discarded packet of explosive and the pliers used by Stauffenberg to set the fuse. The handle of the pliers had been modified so that he could set the fuse one-handed.

A few days later, Stauffenberg was summoned to Rastenburg once again. The plotters knew that this might be their last chance. Stauffenberg spent the evening preparing his report and then went to meet his brother. On the way home he stopped to pray at a Catholic church.

Soon after 6 a.m. on 20th July Stauffenberg and his adjutant, Lieutenant Werner von Haeften, drove out through the Berlin suburbs to Rangsdorf airport. They dared not discuss their mission in front of their driver. At 7 a.m. they were airborne. Stauffenberg's briefcase contained his conference papers with the bomb in between them, wrapped

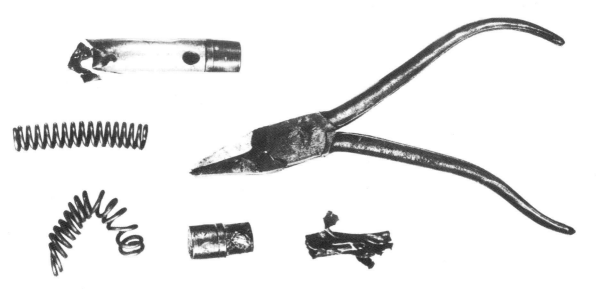

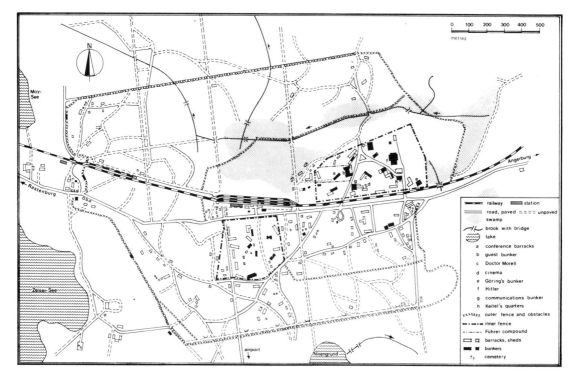

railway ▬▬▬ station
road, paved ══ unpaved
swamp
brook with bridge
lake
a conference barracks
b guest bunker
c Doctor Morell
d cinema
e Göring's bunker
f Hitler
g communications bunker
h Keitel's quarters
×××××× outer fence and obstacles
▬·▬·▬ inner fence
·········· Führer compound
□ □ barracks, sheds
■ ■ bunkers
†† cemetery

The Wolf's Lair at Rastenburg, East Prussia, was in an area of wetland and the Führer compound at its heart was protected by three rings of minefields, pill-boxes and barbed wire, patrolled by guards.

Now in Poland, the Wolf's Lair can be visited by tourists. This photograph shows the bunker marked f on the plan, as it appears today.

in a shirt. Haeften's briefcase contained a second bomb; if the first one proved to be faulty, Stauffenberg would find an excuse to leave the conference to fetch it.

Each bomb weighed about two pounds. They had been made in England, and had silent fuses which would be set off by breaking a glass capsule filled with acid. The acid would dissolve a wire and this would release the firing pin; the timing of the bomb depended on the thickness of the wire. Today's bomb contained the thinnest wire possible; the acid would eat through it in ten minutes. Stauffenberg would break the glass capsule, using a pair of tongs or pliers held in his three remaining fingers.

Rastenburg was 350 miles northeast from Berlin, a flight of just over three hours. When the aircraft touched down, Stauffenberg ordered the pilot to be ready to take them back to Berlin at any moment. The two men then drove the nine miles to Hitler's "Wolf's Lair". The wooded complex was designed in three rings, one within the other. Each ring was protected by minefields, pill-boxes and an electrified barbed-wire fence, and was entered via an S.S. security checkpoint. Even senior officers needed a special pass, valid for only one visit, to enter the inner ring. General Jodl described the place as a cross between a monastery and a concentration camp; it was deathly silent and the sun rarely penetrated the forest.

Stauffenberg and Haeften had no trouble getting in, because they had been summoned by Hitler himself. The problem would be getting out again and hurrying back to Berlin once the bomb had gone off. They were given a good breakfast, and then met General Fellgiebel, Chief of Signals at Rastenburg. He was a key member of the plot; it would be his task to cut off all communications links with the outside world while Stauffenberg escaped.

Shortly after noon Stauffenberg arrived at the quarters of General Keitel, the Chief of the High Command. He was told that Mussolini, the Italian dictator who had recently fled from Rome, would be arriving by train at 2.30 p.m. to see Hitler; the conference was therefore running about half an hour earlier than Stauffenberg had expected. His report would have to be brief. Stauffenberg realized that he would also have to be quick with his bomb.

He now discovered that the conference was taking place not in an underground bunker but in a room partly above ground. He would need to plant the bomb very close to Hitler, to be sure of maximum impact. He summarised his report to Keitel and was told that they must begin the three-minute walk to the conference room immediately. Stauffenberg was careful to leave his cap and belt behind; a moment later he muttered to Keitel that he had forgotten them and hurried back alone. He broke the bomb's acid capsule, collected the "forgotten" items and was soon back at Keitel's side, calm and cheerful. Keitel was annoyed at the delay but not suspicious about the length of time that Stauffenberg had been away. A man so badly injured would need a little extra time to put on his belt.

The two men entered the conference building. Stauffenberg told the sergeant-major operating the telephone switchboard that he was expecting an urgent call from Berlin with important information for his report; he made sure that Keitel heard him. Again Keitel does not seem to have been suspicious, although it would have been unusual even for a senior officer to leave Hitler's presence without special permission.

They were late as Keitel had feared. When they entered the conference room, the meeting had already begun. Four minutes of the ten-minute bomb fuse would already have been eaten away. Keitel took his place next to Hitler; Stauffenberg put the briefcase in position and quietly left the room. But he did not go to the telephone. He walked rapidly past the switchboard and out of the building towards Fellgiebel's office two hundred metres away. Haeften was waiting with the spare bomb; the car was ready for departure.

Hitler in the conference barracks at Rastenburg. It was in this room that Claus von Stauffenberg planted the bomb in his unsuccessful assassination attempt on 20th July, 1944.

Stauffenberg lit a cigarette and waited, staring at the conference building. He was not to know that at that moment Colonel Brandt, unaware of the bomb beneath him, was moving the briefcase round to the other side of the table leg. A moment later the bomb exploded. There was a roar of smoke and flame. Bodies came hurtling out of the windows. People screaming and shouting. With a hasty farewell to Fellgiebel, Stauffenberg leapt into the car. He and Haeften drove quickly away.

Plan of the room in which the bomb exploded.

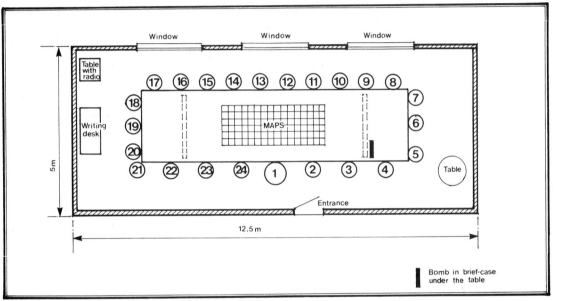

1 Adolf Hitler.

2 General Heusinger, chief of the operations branch of the General Staff of the Army and deputy of the chief of the General Staff.

3 Luftwaffe General Korten, chief of the General Staff of the air force; died of his injuries.

4 Colonel Brandt of the General Staff. Heusinger's deputy; died of his injuries.

5 Luftwaffe General Bodenschatz, Göring's liaison officer in the Führer headquarters; severely wounded.

6 General Schmundt, chief adjutant of the armed forces with the Führer; died later of his injuries.

7 Lieut. Col. Borgmann of the General Staff, adjutant of the Führer; severely injured.

8 Rear Admiral von Puttkamer, naval adjutant of the Führer; lightly injured.

9 Stenographer Berger; killed on the spot.

10 Naval Captain Assmann, admiralty staff officer in the armed forces operations staff.

11 General Scherff, special commissioner of the Führer for the writing of military history; lightly injured.

12 General Buhle, chief of the army staff at the armed forces high command; lightly injured.

13 Rear Admiral Voss, representative of the commander-in-chief of the navy in the Führer headquarters.

14 S.S. group leader Fegelein, representative of the Waffen S.S. in the Führer headquarters.

15 Colonel von Below of the General Staff, air force adjutant of the Führer.

16 S.S. Hauptsturmführer Günsche, adjutant of the Führer.

17 Stenographer Hagen.

18 Lieut. Col. von John of the General Staff, Keitel's adjutant.

19 Major Büchs of the General Staff, Jodl's adjutant.

20 Lieut. Col. Weizenegger of the General Staff, Keitel's adjutant.

21 Ministerial Counsellor von Sonnleithner, Foreign Office representative in the Führer headquarters.

22 General Warlimont, deputy chief of the armed forces operations staff; slight concussion.

23 General Jodl, chief of the armed forces operations staff; lightly wounded.

24 Field Marshal Keitel, chief of the armed forces High Command.

Rastenburg: afternoon

Fellgiebel stood outside his office, staring at the ruined conference barracks. He said later that the damage was so devastating that it looked as if a 155 mm shell had scored a direct hit. Flames and smoke were gathering strength inside. The conference table had been blown to pieces; the ceiling had fallen in on top of everyone. One man who had been blasted straight out through the windows had run to get help. Surely no-one else in there could be alive.

Other soldiers ran towards the building. There was great confusion. Then, to Fellgiebel's utter horror, Hitler staggered out, holding on to Keitel's arm. Very badly shaken but not severely injured, he was barely recognizable. His hair was on fire and his legs were burned. Falling wreckage had bruised and temporarily paralysed his right arm. His eardrums had been punctured, and a falling beam had cut his back; his

Hermann Göring examines the damage at Rastenburg. On the right is the heavy oak table that saved Hitler's life.

buttocks were so badly bruised that he said afterwards that he had had "a backside like a baboon". His trousers were in tatters. But he was alive. Colonel Brandt, in moving the briefcase, had unwittingly saved his life. Brandt himself had died in the explosion; the other victims were two generals and a secretary.

Fellgiebel wondered desperately what to do. The plan was for him to send a message to the plotters in Berlin telling them whether or not to take over the city. But only "stop" or "go" signals had been arranged; there was no coded message to indicate that a bomb had gone off but had failed to kill Hitler. And there was no way of contacting Stauffenberg in his aircraft. Having contacted Berlin, Fellgiebel was supposed to blow up the whole Rastenburg communications network. The S.S. would then be unable to contact units elsewhere.

There has always been some doubt as to what, if anything, Fellgiebel actually did. Historians who are sympathetic to him have suggested that poor lines and war damage had delayed all calls between Rastenburg and Berlin that day. This would explain why Fellgiebel failed to contact Berlin as soon as Stauffenberg had left. They also state that he received a call from Berlin shortly after 1 p.m. and that he gave the conspirators a very guarded account of what had happened, not daring to say whether Hitler was dead or alive. Some also say that he then ordered all calls to be blocked, and that a number of lines were actually cut.

Other writers believe that once Fellgiebel saw that Hitler was alive, he lost heart, decided to send no message and to obey Hitler's order to keep quiet about the whole affair. They also believe that the call from Berlin came through much later, at about 3.30 p.m. By this time the plotters there would have been desperate for information and would be anxious to know why he had not contacted them. We shall never know the precise time of the call and whether or not it was actually Fellgiebel to whom they spoke. Arguments about whether or not Fellgiebel should be blamed for letting the other plotters down will also continue, partly because we do not know enough about the mechanics of the Rastenburg communications system.

What we can be sure about is that the plotters never had adequate control of the system, and that they never planned in sufficient detail to achieve that control. Destroying all links between Rastenburg and the outside world would have meant blowing up equipment housed in several underground bunkers. Fellgiebel claimed later that he had warned his fellow-plotters that this would need fifteen to twenty men, but that he had merely been left to do the best he could. Nazi leaders certainly believed that this was a crucial mistake. Goebbels observed: "To think that these revolutionaries weren't even smart enough to cut the telephone wires – my little daughter would have thought of that!"

Meanwhile the conspirators in Berlin were still wondering what to do.

*   *   *   *   *   *   *

Stauffenberg and Haeften had hurried to get out of Rastenburg as quickly as possible. Guards had closed all checkpoints as soon as they heard the explosion; in less than two minutes, the car reached the first barrier. Stauffenberg jumped out and demanded to use the duty officer's telephone. With the officer present he telephoned – or pretended to telephone – someone; then he put the 'phone down and told the man that he was allowed to pass. It was a complete bluff, but it succeeded. The officer noted the time in his log, let Stauffenberg through and telephoned the guards at the next checkpoint to tell them to do the same. At the outer perimeter things were more difficult. The S.S. guard at this final barrier had already been doubled, and a stubborn sergeant-major refused to allow Stauffenberg through without speaking personally to a senior camp officer, Captain von Moellendorff. Stauffenberg 'phoned him: "I'm in a hurry. General Fromm is waiting for me at the airfield." This was a bluff too; Stauffenberg knew perfectly well that Fromm was in Berlin. The lie succeeded.

As the car sped on towards the airport, Haeften hurriedly took the second bomb to pieces. He tossed the parts out along the side of the road as Stauffenberg constantly urged the driver to accelerate. The airfield authorities had not yet received any alarm, and the pilot already had the engines warming up when they arrived. They took off soon after 1 p.m.

As the plane flew back to Berlin, Stauffenberg had three hours in which to wonder just how much information Fellgiebel would have been able to send to the plotters there. The plane had no radio and so he could not contact Ölbricht himself. He was still confident that Hitler was dead. As soon as they landed at Rangsdorf at 3.45 p.m., he rushed to the airport telephone to contact the others.

*   *   *   *   *   *   *

Back at Rastenburg Hitler had rapidly taken command of the situation despite his injuries. No-one was quite sure at first precisely what had happened. Hitler himself thought that an enemy plane might have dropped a bomb in a sneak attack. General Jodl, who had been standing close to Hitler at the conference table and whose head had been cut by a falling chandelier, thought that builders might have planted a time bomb under the floor of the room – this would explain the deep hole in the middle of the wreckage. Colonel Brandt might well have been able to guess what had happened – if he had not been killed in the explosion.

Hitler gave immediate orders that the assassination attempt was to be kept as secret as possible, while Himmler, the head of the S.S., quickly ordered his office in Berlin to send a team of detectives to investigate. This was certainly one call which Fellgiebel failed to prevent. From that moment on, the S.S. controlled all messages in and out of the Wolf's Lair; communications were closed down for over two hours during the afternoon, which would strengthen the view that the plotters in Berlin got no news before 3.30 p.m.

At first, no-one remembered that Stauffenberg had crept out of the room just before the bomb went off. It was assumed that he had been among the seriously injured and that he had been rushed to hospital. But as Himmler's S.S. got to work, it became clear that Stauffenberg's movements had been highly suspicious. A check at the hospital revealed that he was not there. The sergeant who had been on the switchboard in the conference building revealed that Stauffenberg had rushed past him just before the bomb exploded. Others remembered his putting his briefcase under the table. The checkpoint guards gave details of his speedy departure for the airport. It would not be long before the police found parts of the second bomb on the verges of the airport road. Witnesses at the airport reported Stauffenberg's hurried take-off for Berlin. Himmler unsuccessfully tried to order that he be arrested as he landed at Rangsdorf, but this was one call which Fellgiebel may have been able to frustrate.

Hitler and his fellow officers still assumed that Stauffenberg had acted alone. They had as yet no inkling of a group of plotters in Berlin and they had other pressing matters to deal with. Mussolini was due to arrive at Rastenburg that afternoon. His train had been delayed and this gave Hitler, who was strangely calm in the hours immediately after the explosion, time to recover from its immediate effects.

Hitler shows Mussolini the damage caused by the Rastenburg bomb. The Italian dictator arrived at Rastenburg on a pre-arranged visit shortly after the attempt on Hitler's life.

Mussolini arrived at 4 p.m. Most of Italy had now fallen to Allied troops; he looked much older than his sixty years. Hitler must have looked a good deal worse as he stood on the platform waiting for the train to arrive. It was a hot and steamy day, but he was wrapped in a heavy cloak to lessen the shivering caused by shock. His burnt hair had been cut away

and cotton wool stuck out of his damaged ears. His right arm was in a sling. He moved very slowly. Although they did not know it, it was to be the last meeting between the two dictators.

It took less than three minutes to drive from the station to Hitler's personal quarters and then to see the wreckage. "Only a short while ago the greatest good fortune in my life took place," declared Hitler. "I was standing here by this table; the bomb went off just in front of my feet . . . . Having escaped death in so extraordinary a way, I am now more than ever convinced that the great cause which I serve will survive its present perils and everything be brought to a good end." Mussolini was horrified as he heard the story and was shown Hitler's tattered uniform. He agreed that it had been a miracle.

At 5 p.m. the two men sat down to tea. Himmler had already been sent to Berlin. Hitler had now begun to suspect that there was some kind of plot there, too, and wanted to know the details. Many of the other leading Nazis had heard news of the bomb by now, and had rushed to Hitler's side. Mussolini watched, embarrassed, as they all began to blame each other for recent setbacks. Admiral Dönitz, head of the Navy, accused the Army of treachery. Göring said the Airforce would save Germany from the terrible situation which Army incompetence had caused. Martin Bormann, a leading Nazi Party official, implied that the Party would save Hitler from the failures of everyone else. A separate argument broke out between Göring and Ribbentrop over German foreign policy.

During most of this argument, Hitler sat quietly swallowing his pills and sucking throat lozenges. Heavy rain began to beat against the windows. Suddenly he rose from his chair and vowed revenge on those who had tried to kill him. "I will crush and destroy the criminals who have dared to oppose me," he shrieked. "I'll put their wives and children into concentration camps and show them no mercy . . . . These traitors deserve death and this is what they shall have. They will be exterminated for once and for all."

Mussolini left Rastenburg shortly before 6 p.m., deeply depressed by what he had seen. Hitler said goodbye at the station, and then demanded to know where Himmler was, forgetting that he had sent him off to Berlin only an hour before. He grabbed a telephone and ordered the S.S. in Berlin to shoot anyone who was the least suspect. It was not an empty threat; he meant what he said.

Berlin: afternoon

Killing Hitler at Rastenburg was only the first stage in the July Plot. It is true that the plotters saw his death as essential if they were to be sure of success, but his assassination alone would not mean that power would fall into their hands. It was vital for them to seize control of Germany's capital, Berlin, as quickly as possible while confusion and uncertainty were widespread and before any other leading Nazi had had time to take over the government. With luck, Goebbels, Himmler and the rest might well get involved in a long power struggle among themselves.

Once Stauffenberg's bomb had gone off, the Plot's success therefore depended on speedy action by some of his brother officers. There had been pockets of resistance to Hitler in the Army as a whole ever since he had come to power in 1933 – resistance which grew with the war setbacks in Russia in 1942-3. A number of officers were also appalled at the cruelty of the S.S. in the countries which Germany had occupied since 1938, and against the Jews in Germany and elsewhere. (This theme is explored in more detail on pages 48-52.)

Stauffenberg counted on support from three key groups. One of these groups was on the Russian front itself, headed by Tresckow. Tresckow had tried unsuccessfully in 1942 to persuade some of his superiors to join in a military takeover in which Hitler would be arrested and brought to trial. He had also master-minded several attempts on Hitler's life in 1943, including smuggling a time bomb (which failed to go off) on to Hitler's aircraft. But none of the front-line generals could be persuaded to dare to desert Hitler. Tresckow therefore had to admit that the best chance of success lay in assassinating Hitler in Germany. Shortly before 20th July he urged Stauffenberg to act soon. "Should it fail," he said, "we will still have to act in Berlin. It is . . . a question of whether the Resistance has dared to make the decisive move before the eyes of the world and of history . . ."

Stauffenberg also counted on support from France. Here resistance groups within the German Army had been trying to persuade the German war hero, General Erwin Rommel, to present Hitler with an ultimatum: the war must be ended or he would be arrested and tried; there was to be a truce in the

West, and all occupied territories were to be evacuated. On 15th July Rommel wrote a long letter to Hitler, pointing out that the German forces were fighting against overwhelming odds. He also wrote: "I must beg you to draw the proper conclusions without delay." He also told a fellow-officer: "I have given him his last chance. If he does not take it, we will act." But two days later Rommel was severely wounded in an Allied air raid and was sent home to Germany to recover. The full ultimatum seems never to have been sent, but Rommel's letter, and two very hostile meetings which he had had with Hitler in the previous month, were to cost him dearly later on. The removal from France of Rommel was a severe blow to the conspirators there; their plans for open resistance to the Führer had had the support of the Army Commander in France, General von Stülpnagel, but the new Commander-in-Chief on the Western Front, General von Kluge, was prepared to help only "in the event of the attempt being a success".

Field Marshal Erwin Rommel (centre) with General Blaskowitz (left) and Field Marshal von Runstedt (right) in Paris, 1944.

By 20th July Stauffenberg therefore had a good deal of evidence that support would follow Hitler's death. But he could not be sure how strong that support would be if Hitler survived or did not die at once. As he flew back from

Rastenburg he knew that many potential supporters both in Russia and in France were likely to come out into the open only if events in Germany itself were already running his way.

Support for Stauffenberg from a third group, the Army in Germany, was therefore crucial. Here his main ally was General Friedrich Ölbricht, Chief of Staff and Deputy

General Friedrich Ölbricht, Deputy Commander of the Home (Reserve) Army and one of Stauffenberg's co-conspirators. Together they had planned "Operation Valkyrie" which would enable the Army to take control of major German cities after Hitler's death. He was executed with Stauffenberg in the courtyard of the War Ministry on the evening of 20th July, 1944.

Commander of the Home (or Reserve) Army. In this role, Ölbricht was responsible for all troops needed for garrison or replacement purposes in Germany, and he was able to place supporters of the opposition in key jobs in Berlin and other major German cities – men who would take speedy control of these cities after Hitler's death.

After the failure of Tresckow's bomb in 1943, Ölbricht and Stauffenberg had begun planning "Operation Valkyrie". Hitler was persuaded that the very large number of foreign labourers now working in armaments and other factories in Germany posed a grave potential threat to him because they might stage a series of revolts in Berlin and other major cities. In fact, such a revolt was unlikely, but Hitler was suspicious enough by this time to see plots everywhere and he readily agreed to detailed preparations being worked out for the Reserve Army to take over all major cities in such a crisis. "Valkyrie" thus provided a perfect cover for the conspirators to lay plans which, far from being designed to protect Hitler, were actually aimed against him.

Speed of action would be crucial, especially in Berlin itself where S.S. and airforce units loyal to Hitler would outnumber the Reserve Army troops. Stauffenberg had won over the head of the Berlin police force, which was now likely to support the plotters, but he also believed that it would be essential to seize all government ministers and broadcasting stations within two hours. Goebbels and leading S.S. officers would have to be arrested within the same period while, it was assumed, Fellgiebel would have cut off communications from Rastenburg. The plotters would then send messages, which had already been prepared, to all Home Army generals and to troop commanders on the Western and Eastern fronts and in occupied countries, declaring that a new, non-Nazi government had been set up in Berlin. The whole revolt would have to be over within a single day if the conspirators were to be sure of support from generals in Russia and France, and if Göring and Himmler were not to be able to rally pro-Nazi troops for a civil war. General Ludwig Beck, who had retired in 1938 in protest at Hitler's war policies and who had joined the conspiracy, was to be the new Head of State, and Field Marshal von Witzleben would be the new Army Commander-in-Chief.

There was one further problem. Ölbricht's immediate superior, General Fritz Fromm, the Commander of the Home Army, was the only man who could normally give the order for Operation Valkyrie to be put into effect. For over a year, the plotters had tried to persuade Fromm to join them: now they felt that they could be certain of his support only if and when he was sure that the revolt had been successful.

General Friedrich Fromm, Commander of the German Home Army. The plotters were never sure how far they could trust him.

As his aircraft prepared to touch down at Rangsdorf, Stauffenberg must have realized only too clearly that everything now depended on how much the plotters in Berlin had managed to achieve during the afternoon, on how many of the doubtfuls had actually joined them, and on whether support would come from other areas.

*   *   *   *   *   *   *

When his plane landed at 3.45 p.m., Stauffenberg could find no car waiting for him. He hurried to telephone Ölbricht at the War Office and was appalled to discover that very little action had so far been taken. The information from Rastenburg had been indistinct and sketchy; the message had not said whether Hitler was alive or dead. The orders to put Operation Valkyrie into effect had not yet been sent out; no troops had been mobilized. Radio, telephone and telegraph networks had not yet been seized. Although it was vital for Beck and Witzleben, as Germany's new "leaders", to broadcast to the civilian population and the armed forces as soon as possible, the plotters' headquarters had not been wired for such a purpose. No orders had been sent out to commanders in other cities.

There seemed to have been very little sense of urgency; Beck and Witzleben had not even arrived yet, and Ölbricht – anxious, no doubt, not to put Valkyrie into effect too soon, as he had done five days earlier – had enjoyed a leisurely lunch with a fellow general, toasting the success of the Plot with a bottle of wine. Stauffenberg assured the plotters that Hitler was dead and urged Ölbricht to launch Valkyrie at once. He then raced to the War Office.

Meanwhile messages by teleprinter and telephone were at last sent out to local commanders, announcing that Hitler was dead and that Witzleben was now head of the armed forces. Not all the staff at the War Office were told of Hitler's "death", and some of those who did receive the information were far from delighted by it. A few began secretly to send out messages for arms and ammunition.

Some of the orders being despatched were in the name of General Fromm, Ölbricht's commander, although Fromm knew nothing about it so far. Ölbricht now informed him that Fellgiebel had telephoned to report Hitler's death, and he urged Fromm to take command of Valkyrie. The plotters were confident that local commanders would obey Fromm's orders without question. But Fromm would not be bulldozed into rapid action. He demanded to talk to Keitel at Rastenburg. Ölbricht, confident that Fellgiebel would have cut off communications, boldly picked up the 'phone and asked for an emergency call. He passed the 'phone to Fromm. The conversation which followed showed that Ölbricht's bluff had gone disastrously wrong; to his horror, he realized that Keitel had come on the line almost immediately.

"What's happening at General Headquarters?" asked Fromm. "There are the wildest rumours here in Berlin."

"What do they say is happening?" replied Keitel. "Everything's normal here." "I've just had a report that the Führer's been assassinated," he was told. "Nonsense," declared Keitel. "It's quite true that an attempt has been made on his life. Fortunately, it failed. The Führer's alive and only slightly injured. But where, by the way, is your Chief of Staff, Colonel Count von Stauffenberg?" "Stauffenberg's not got back yet."

The conversation ended. Fromm immediately told Ölbricht that Operation Valkyrie was not to be put into operation. Ölbricht returned to his office, stunned. Shortly afterwards, Stauffenberg got back. It was now a little after 4.30 p.m. Beck had also arrived by now; Ölbricht and he confronted Stauffenberg with Keitel's information. Stauffenberg assured them that Keitel must be lying because he wanted to play for time. "I saw it myself," Stauffenberg kept repeating. "It's impossible that anyone could have survived." Beck agreed with him that there was no alternative but to go ahead with Valkyrie whether Hitler was dead or alive. It was too late to go back now.

Ölbricht took Stauffenberg to Fromm's office. "I myself set off the bomb and I myself saw the Führer's body carried out of the hut," he told Fromm. Ölbricht added that despite Fromm's orders, Operation Valkyrie was now in full swing. Fromm was furious. "Count Stauffenberg," he declared, "the attempt has failed. You must shoot yourself at once." Stauffenberg refused, and Fromm declared that he and Ölbricht were under arrest. "It is we who are arresting you," they replied. There was a brief struggle and Fromm was put under armed guard. The telephone lines in his room were cut.

Events were now moving very fast. Word came that Hitler's survival was to be announced on national radio at any minute, but the plotters still made no move to seize the radio station. The Berlin police chief was ready to do this, but received no orders from the War Office. Stauffenberg did manage to put through a call to Paris, urging immediate action there, and General Stülpnagel arrested 1200 S.S. officers and men before nightfall. But the plotters' attention was increasingly being distracted from the vital tasks by other, minor crises.

General von Kortzfleisch, the District Commander in Berlin, arrived in person to find out what was happening. He demanded to see Fromm; Beck had to explain the position to him. He flatly refused to join the plotters, and had to be put under guard with Fromm. An S.S. officer, Oberführer Piffraeder, suddenly appeared. He had been ordered from

Rastenburg to arrest Stauffenberg quickly and quietly, but his superiors there had not been able to give him any other details and so he had no idea what was going on and had brought only two men with him. These three men were also arrested. Some of the conspirators wanted them shot so that they would not observe the plot being carried out, but Stauffenberg rejected this. He was probably mistaken.

By 6 p.m. it was clear that Hitler was alive. The telephones at Rastenburg, far from being cut off, were sending a stream of messages from Keitel to local commanders, instructing them that any orders from the War Office were to be ignored. Beck and Stauffenberg had to work tirelessly to encourage those conspirators who began to lose heart, and to assure those who telephoned the War Office that the Army under Witzleben was in control of the country. Not all were convinced; one prominent commander, Field Marshal von Kluge, promised to call back in half an hour to say whether or not he would support the plot. He did not do so. For Stauffenberg and his fellow conspirators, the future looked very grim indeed.

Berlin: evening

One of the key tasks in Operation Valkyrie was the seizure of government ministers and the S.S. headquarters in Berlin. If these buildings could be secured, all might not yet be lost for the plotters. Shortly after 4 p.m. General von Hase, the City Commandant of Berlin and a member of the conspiracy, telephoned the commander of one of his crack batallions, Major Otto Remer, and ordered him to report at once to Hase's headquarters.

Dr Josef Goebbels, Hitler's Minister for Popular Enlightenment and Propaganda, addressing a meeting in Berlin. His prompt action in Berlin in the hours after the plot was crucial in causing the downfall of the conspirators.

Remer had been newly appointed, but the plotters had chosen him carefully. He was known to be a brave soldier who had won a number of decorations and he was thought to be uninvolved in politics and therefore likely to obey the orders of his military commander without question. Hase told Remer that Hitler was dead and that the S.S. was trying to seize control of the government. Remer was ordered to seize a number of key buildings, and had done so by 5.30 p.m. He was also ordered to arrest Josef Goebbels, the Propaganda Minister and the senior Nazi minister then in Berlin.

Remer entered the Propaganda Ministry with twenty men, ordering them to come and fetch him if he did not return from Goebbels' office within a few minutes. Goebbels had recently received orders from Hitler at Rastenburg to transmit an emergency radio announcement that Hitler was alive and well; he knew little of the detailed events there, and would have had no inkling of what was currently happening in Berlin, but for the sudden arrival of an unexpected visitor shortly after Hitler's 'phone call. The visitor, a writer and lecturer named Captain Hans Hagen, was a keen Nazi who had been with Remer when Remer first received the order to alert his men and report to his superior officer. Hagen was also convinced that earlier in the day he had seen Field Marshal von Brauchitsch, an officer long since retired, in full uniform, driving through Berlin in an army car. Hagen had not, in fact, seen anything of the sort; Brauchitsch was not in Berlin that day. But the fact that Hagen *thought* he had seen him convinced him that a seizure of power by the Army under Brauchitsch was taking place. Once again, the plotters were very unlucky. Remer had agreed that Hagen should tell Goebbels all he knew.

Goebbels, who had been irritated by Hagen's sudden arrival as he was trying to draft his radio broadcast, looked out of his window and saw army troops taking up positions all round the ministry. He was quickly convinced that Hagen was right. Hagen left, and Remer and his adjutant entered Goebbels' office shortly afterwards with pistols drawn. Goebbels had to think fast. He reminded Remer that, as an officer, he had sworn an oath of loyalty to Hitler. When Remer replied that Hitler was dead, Goebbels picked up the telephone and put through an urgent call to Rastenburg. Hitler himself was on the line in a minute or two. Remer recognized the husky voice at once and snapped to attention. Hitler told him to crush the plot immediately and to obey only the commands of Goebbels, or of Himmler whom he had appointed to take over the Home Army and who was now on his way to the capital. He also promoted Remer to Colonel on the spot. Remer did not hesitate. Within a short time his troops had withdrawn from the ministries and were occupying the Home Army's headquarters instead. He had set off himself to find out where the plotters' headquarters was situated, so that he could arrest them. They did not know for some time that he had changed sides.

Goebbels' radio announcement that Hitler was alive was a terrible blow to the plotters. Stauffenberg immediately sent a teleprinter message to as many army commanders as he could contact, denying the fact. But the damage had been done, and in cities like Prague and Vienna where commanders had begun to arrest S.S. and Nazi party leaders, they were already putting their plans into reverse. By 8.20 p.m. they were receiving more specific messages on the teleprinter from Keitel at Rastenburg. These said that Himmler was now head of the Home Army; only orders from him or from Keitel himself were to be obeyed. Army orders from Fromm or Witzleben should be ignored. Worse still for the plotters, the Commandant of the Panzer tank school in Berlin, who had been ordered to send his tanks into the city in support of the plot, came to the War Office and refused to take orders from Ölbricht. He, too, had sensed that the plot was failing, and he had to be locked up with Fromm and the other prisoners. So inefficient was the guard on him that he was later able to escape from the building; so were three officers of Fromm's staff, who went off to look for help.

Field Marshal von Witzleben, the man whom the plotters had chosen as the new army chief, finally arrived at the War Office in full uniform just after 8 p.m. He had spent the day at army headquarters outside the city. He knew at once that the plot had failed. "A fine mess, this," he declared. The plotters began arguing amongst themselves, and three-quarters of an hour later Witzleben stormed out of the building and back to his country estate. There was worse to come. Soon after 9 p.m. there was another radio announcement. Hitler himself would broadcast to the German people later that evening.

*   *   *   *   *   *   *

By 9 p.m. the plot was doomed to failure. General Reinecke – a fervent Nazi – and the S.S. had taken command of all Berlin troops and were said to be preparing to storm the War

Office. In Berlin and other cities, commanders who had either pledged support for the plot or who had decided to support it as soon as success seemed likely, were busily and noisily showing their support for Hitler. They included a group of Ölbricht's junior officers who called on him at 10.30 p.m. and demanded to know precisely what was happening. Ölbricht told them and they left him. Twenty minutes later they were back – with weapons – insisting on seeing Ölbricht again. One of them pointed a tommy-gun at Ölbricht and demanded to see Fromm. There was a brief scuffle, and Stauffenberg looked into the office to see who was causing the noise. Too late he tried to escape and was shot in his remaining arm.

During the next few minutes this group loyal to Hitler rounded up most of the plotters. Fromm appeared soon afterwards, waving a revolver. He would need to act quickly if he was to cover up the fact that he had known about the possibility of a plot; Himmler would be back in Berlin by now and there could be some very awkward questions to answer. "Lay down your weapons," he ordered to the conspirators. "You surely won't ask me, your old commanding officer to do that?" said Beck. He reached quietly for his own revolver.

General Ludwig Beck, ex-chief of the Army General Staff. He warned Hitler in 1938 that aggressive German actions towards Czechoslovakia would lead to war with Britain – and was proved wrong when Neville Chamberlain made an agreement with the Führer at Munich.

31

"Keep it pointed towards yourself," shouted Fromm. "At a time like this," continued Beck, "it is the old days I remember." Fromm told him to get it over quickly. Beck, determined to commit suicide, pointed the revolver at his temple and fired. The bullet merely scratched him and drew blood. He collapsed into a chair in deep shock.

When Beck pleaded to be allowed to make a second attempt, Fromm agreed. To the others Fromm said: "Gentlemen, if you have any letters to write, I'll give you a few more minutes." Ölbricht and another officer wrote notes for their wives. Stauffenberg, his arm bleeding heavily, lay slumped in a chair. Fromm announced to all those in the room that he had held an emergency court martial and that Ölbricht, Stauffenberg and their adjutants had been sentenced to death "in the name of the Führer". The sentence would be carried out at once.

The four men were led downstairs into the courtyard. An army car stood there, its headlights dimmed to obey the blackout regulations. There was some shouting from the ten soldiers who formed the firing squad; they wanted the prisoners to hurry up because of the threat of an air raid. Stauffenberg died shouting "Long live our sacred Germany!" Upstairs, Beck was asking for another weapon. "If it doesn't work this time, please help me," he said. He fired the shot, again unsuccessfully, and a sergeant, who found him unconscious, finished him off with a bullet in the neck.

*　　*　　*　　*　　*　　*　　*

Just after 1 a.m. on 21st July, Hitler made his radio broadcast. "You should know that I am unhurt and well," he said, "and you should know of a crime unparalleled in German history. A very small clique of ambitious, irresponsible, senseless and stupid officers had concocted a plot to eliminate me . . . . It is a gang of criminal elements which will be destroyed without mercy. We shall settle accounts in the manner to which we National Socialists are accustomed."

A great many accounts were to be settled over the next few months. But although Hitler did not know it yet, Stauffenberg and Ölbricht had been dealt with already. The July Plot had failed.

THE INVESTIGATION

Why kill Hitler?
1 Events in Germany, 1918-44

Hitler's early life When Adolf Hitler joined the German Workers' Party in September 1919 it had only a handful of members and virtually no funds. Within a short time Hitler had merged the Party into his own new National Socialist German Workers' (Nazi) Party and he was its undisputed leader. His word was law, even to his most senior followers, and he took every major decision. If, as the plotters believed, Nazism was leading Germany to disaster, the only way to prevent that disaster was to remove the leader himself. In a dictatorship with a strong secret police, this could not be done by persuasion or votes in parliament – only by force and with great secrecy.

By any standards, Hitler was remarkable. Born in 1889 in an obscure valley region in Austria, he was the son of a minor civil servant. He drifted into Vienna in 1906, hoping to attend either the Academy of Art or the School of Architecture, but was rejected by both and spent the next few years scraping a living together by casual work as a housepainter or station porter. He also made a little money through faking pictures. Even at that stage, he argued passionately about politics in cafés, but was never prepared to listen to a viewpoint different from his own. Above all, he believed that life had been very unfair to him and that his talents were unrecognized. He resented his poverty and envied the rich people of Vienna. Those who were Jewish as well as rich were a special target for his hatred.

Rejected on health grounds for Austrian military service, he moved to Munich in Germany in 1913. He now believed that the Germans had been destined by history to become the master-race of Europe, that these "Aryan" people had made all the valuable achievements of the past, and that they had both the right and the duty to rule the Europe of the future.

Above all, their blood must not be "polluted" by inter-marriage with inferior races such as the Jews and the Slav groups of Eastern Europe.

Hitler and the First World War

When war broke out in 1914, Hitler enthusiastically joined the German Army. He rose to the rank of corporal, and was awarded the Iron Cross, First Class. We do not know what he did to earn this, but it was an unusual decoration for such a junior soldier. Temporarily blinded in a gas attack, he heard in hospital the shattering news of the sudden collapse and defeat of Germany in 1918. He refused to accept it, believing that Germany had been "stabbed in the back" by socialist politicians and Jews. Within six months, the victorious powers (including Britain) had forced Germany to accept the

An S.A. souvenir woodcut with a message from Hitler: "What you are, you are through me. But what I am, I am only through you."

humiliating treaty of Versailles. Germany's lands were divided into two by a Polish "corridor", her colonies were confiscated, she was forced to admit that the war had been her fault, and was to pay £6,600 million ("reparations") to her conquerors in compensation. Hitler vowed revenge.

Hitler's political career, 1919-33

In the highly charged atmosphere of the early 1920s Hitler quickly proved to be a magnetic political figure. When he was put in charge of propaganda for the German Workers' Party within a short time he was not only its leader but was addressing audiences of thousands. The party adopted the crooked cross "swastika" as its emblem. Ernst Röhm, a thuggish ex-Army captain, was a useful ally in recruiting ex-servicemen into the *Sturmabteilung* or S.A. – a uniformed, semi-military organization. There was a party newspaper named *Völkischer Beobachter*, and Hitler recruited a number of people with money and influence into the Party to pay for it. He showed himself to be a brilliant communicator. His speeches always contained the same messages: the treaty of Versailles must be overthrown, world domination by socialists and Jews must be prevented, Germany must be made great again.

In 1923 Germany fell behind with her "reparations" payments to the Allies. France invaded to seize coal in compensation. The value of the German currency, the *Mark*, collapsed. Hitler saw his chance, and led a march on the centre of Munich to seize power. (Munich was the capital of Bavaria, a state which had become a full part of the German Empire only fifty years earlier and whose state government was often at loggerheads with the national government in

As the value of the Mark plummeted, companies used laundry baskets to pick up loads of freshly printed money to pay their wages. As soon as the workers were paid (often daily) there was a rush to the shops to buy groceries before prices rose further. There is at least one instance of someone putting down a laundry basket full of money while he opened the door of a shop, and the laundry basket being stolen while the money was left on the pavement at his feet.

Berlin.) But Hitler's attempted take-over was a crude operation, poorly thought out, and it made him a talking-point in Europe as the authorities easily crushed it. Hitler was imprisoned – but only for nine months. The lightness of the sentence can be partly explained by the fact that Bavarian judges were notoriously sympathetic to right-wing figures (although they were very hard on communists). But the main reason is the superb performance given by Hitler at his trial. He not only turned the trial into a political triumph by making long and much-publicized speeches to explain his views, but he even persuaded the chief prosecution lawyer to make a number of sympathetic points on his behalf. During the short time he served in prison he wrote a book, *Mein Kampf* ("My Struggle"). He deliberately let the Party collapse to show that without him it would achieve nothing.

The next five years saw little progress for the Nazis. Germany became prosperous again. The Nazis did poorly in elections. Röhm went off to South America. But in 1929 the American stock market on Wall Street, New York, crashed. Much of Germany's recovery had been thanks to American loans. These now stopped, and the *Mark* collapsed once

Ernst Röhm, head of the S.A., with other S.A. leaders.

again. Many Germans became bankrup
promised that if he got power, Germans w
victims of events abroad. Röhm returne
squads began beating up political oppon
The Nazi party began winning la
parliamentary seats.

Hitler takes power

By 1932 it was clear that no political party could hold a parliamentary majority without Hitler's support. The Nazis did not have a majority of seats over all the other parties combined, but Hitler refused to form any government unless he were made head of it. Months of negotiations followed, as Hitler played off one politician against another – particularly Franz von Papen of the Centre Party and General von Schleicher, both of whom briefly held office as Chancellor during 1932. Hitler hoped that one of them could eventually be persuaded to serve under him in a coalition and that one of these two men would convince the President, Field Marshal von Hindenburg, that Hitler could be trusted as Chancellor and head of the government. He was right; in January 1933 Papen agreed to serve as Vice Chancellor under Hitler. A vain man with a greatly exaggerated sense of his own ability, Papen believed that Hitler could easily be controlled. "We have boxed him in," he said. It was a terrible mistake.

Within a month, the Parliament building in Berlin had burned down. The Nazis blamed the Communist party and banned it. During the next year, all other political parties were banned. The Nazis soon controlled the police, the judges, local government and the education system. Non-Nazi teachers lost their jobs; children had to be taught Nazi

Hitler and the Italian Crown Prince watching the Olympic Games. Hitler used the games to establish his respectability in Europe, but was highly annoyed when Jesse Owens, a black American, won four gold medals.

Hitler addressing the 1936 National Socialist party rally at Nuremberg. The columns of light come from searchlights surrounding the parade ground.

The National Socialist party tried to control all aspects of German life. These girls from a Nazi youth group were photographed outside the Reich Chancellery in Berlin in May 1939, cheering Hitler on signing the German/Italian alliance.

ideas and were expected to join the Hitler Youth movement. Goebbels, Hitler's Propaganda Minister, controlled the cinema, radio and newspapers. Books which criticized Nazism were publicly burned and works by Jewish authors were banned. The Trades Unions had lost their independence, and the Nazis had set up their own "Reichschurch" over and above the Catholic and Protestant Churches.

Some Germans did benefit from Nazism. Unemployment fell dramatically as Hitler began a huge programme of motorway building, agricultural schemes and, above all, weapons building. Money for these schemes was borrowed from abroad, and loans frequently remained unpaid long after they were due; Britain, France and America were unwilling to risk another war against Germany if they could avoid it. The Nazis organized sport, leisure activities and holidays for German workers and designed a cheap "People's Car", the Volkswagen. However, Germans were expected to pay for the cars in advance and very few were actually built. The scheme was a swindle, designed to pay for rearmament. In the early years after Hitler came to power the wages of many Germans kept up with price increases, but later on there was another price to be paid for all this: take-home pay was gradually reduced by higher taxes and workers were not allowed to move freely from one job to another. Anyone who dared to criticize the Nazis was unlikely to get a job at all.

Hitler crushes his opponents Between 1933 and 1939 all opposition to Hitler was ruthlessly crushed. The most dramatic example of this ruthlessness was the "Night of the Long Knives" in 1934. For some time Hitler had been building up a secret police force, the S.S. (*Schutzstaffel*), under Heinrich Himmler, as a counter-weight to the Stormtroopers. Hitler felt increasingly threatened by the street violence of Röhm and the S.A. He also wanted to put a stop to their call for more taxes on the rich, because he was afraid that the industrialists would turn against him, and he lived in permanent fear that if the S.A. got out of control, the Army might use this as an excuse for seizing power. The S.A. were therefore wiped out in a carefully planned operation by the S.S., along with a number of Hitler's other political opponents.

The Jews were either forced into exile abroad or terrorized by local mobs who burned their homes and looted their shops. In the later 1930s, laws were passed restricting their education and job opportunities. They were forced to wear distinctive

39

clothing and were herded into special "ghetto" areas of cities or sent off to concentration camps. Long before 1939, Hitler had constructed a reign of terror and had total control of German life.

When war came, the government took even stronger powers over the German people and over the economy. As Hitler occupied large areas of Eastern Europe, Jews and other opponents were increasingly transported to extermination camps, mainly in Poland. Some Germans were revolted by this; others preferred to ignore it. Some were also fearful of Germany's future when war setbacks began. But resistance seemed hopeless; Himmler's secret police were everywhere and any protest was likely to mean immediate arrest. Hitler, constantly fearful that there might be a repeat of the factory strikes and mutinies in the armed forces that had caused collapse in 1918, worked hard to keep up civilian morale through censorship of the newspapers and radio. The German people remained remarkably loyal to him.

For all these reasons, the plotters of 1944 knew that Hitler's death was essential. They had come to hate his brutality. He controlled the Nazi party totally; no other leading Nazi was likely to risk opposing him. Through the S.S. he controlled Germany completely; no civilian revolt was possible, and only the Army had the power to oppose him. His remarkable achievements since 1918 had made it impossible to reason with him; he would never compromise with an opponent. They also believed that his foreign policy was leading Germany to total ruin.

Soon after coming to power the Nazis began to construct "concentration camps" to house political prisoners. Later these prisoners were joined by Jews, gypsies and other "undesirables". This photograph was taken at the camp at Dachau, the first concentration camp to be set up, near Munich, in 1933.

Why kill Hitler?
2 Foreign policy, 1933-44

The cautious early years

The map shows how much land was lost and how Germany was divided in two parts by the Versailles treaty.

Hitler had always been determined to make Germany the master of Europe. When he came to power in 1933 his first aim was to overturn the Versailles treaty. This treaty had placed severe restrictions on both the level and type of German armaments; Germany's Army was to be limited to 100,000, and she was allowed no submarines, tanks or military aircraft. Hitler ignored these curbs, rearming cautiously up to 1935 and much more quickly after that. Britain and France made no significant protest.

It was important in these early years for Hitler to avoid direct conflict with Britain and France. He was anxious to

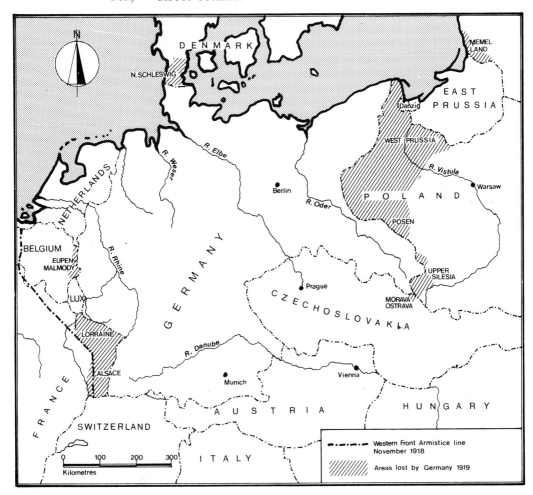

seem reasonable, and demonstrated this by a non-aggression pact with Poland in January 1934. However, at the same time, he took Germany out of the League of Nations and the Geneva disarmament conference. He also encouraged Austrian Nazis in their attempt to seize power in 1934, although strong protest by the Italians (who had much to fear from unification of Germany and Austria) forced him to disown the plot when it failed.

By 1935 Hitler felt strong enough to reintroduce compulsory military service. He was able to persuade the British to negotiate a new naval agreement with him. This not only undermined the Versailles treaty restrictions (which the British now felt had been too harsh), but also caused a rift in Britain's recent agreements with France and Italy. Hitler noted how Britain and France protested when Mussolini invaded Abyssinia in East Africa, but also how they failed to take any effective action against him; they failed to cut off his oil supplies. Hitler was sure that they dreaded the prospect of another war, and would prefer to give in to his demands.

On Saturday, 16 March, 1935 Hitler announced a law establishing universal military conscription, and providing for a peacetime army of twelve corps and 36 divisions (roughly 500,000 men). 17 March, which was Heroes Memorial Day, became a celebration of the death of the Treaty of Versailles and the rebirth of the conscript German Army.

Hitler becomes more daring

Early in 1936 German troops marched into the Rhineland. This was the part of Germany which bordered on French territory, and the victorious Allies at Versailles in 1919 had decided to turn it into a buffer zone where German troops would not be allowed. For a time Allied troops had actually patrolled the bridgeheads between the Rhineland and the rest of Germany, but these soldiers had been withdrawn during the mid-1920s. Hitler calculated, correctly, that the Allies would do nothing even though he was now in direct defiance of the Versailles treaty. He also sent help to General Franco, a fellow-dictator who was fighting against left-wing forces in the Spanish Civil War.

1937 was mainly spent drawing up a Four Year Plan to give Germany her own supplies of all key materials in case of a future war, and to finance increasingly rapid rearmament. At the Hossbach Conference Hitler seemed finally to reject the idea of counting Britain as an ally and declared that Germany must win all the new territory she needed within six years.

In 1938 Hitler openly defied the Allies. Declaring that Austria was a German-speaking country and could therefore

Nazi troops crossing into Austria, 11th March, 1938.

be considered as part of the *Volk* (or German nation), he ordered German troops to enter Austria in March and the two countries were united. A referendum held soon afterwards gave a vote of 99.75% in favour of Hitler – or so he claimed. This was perhaps not surprising as the S.S. had arrested 79,000 people in Vienna alone. Hitler gained another 100,000 men for his army and large quantities of iron, steel and foreign currency. Again the Allies made no effective protest and again Hitler was merely encouraged to become more daring.

Five months later Hitler demanded that the Sudetenland, the area of North and West Czechoslovakia in which most of the population spoke German, should be given to Germany, and stirred up a revolt amongst Nazis there. Hitler hated the Czechs, believing them to be racially inferior, and he wanted to get his hands on their excellent industrial plant, notably the Skoda steelworks. The Czechs expected support from Britain, and from France with whom they had a treaty. The British Prime Minister, Neville Chamberlain, fearing a war and knowing that British rearmament had only just begun, doggedly believed that Hitler was a reasonable man with whom he could negotiate. He flew to meet him three times. At a final international conference in Munich, Hitler was given nearly everything he wanted in the Sudetenland. Although the Allies announced that they would protect the rest of Czechoslovakia, Hitler occupied Prague with little protest only six months later.

Mussolini, Hitler, Daladier and Chamberlain in Munich during the talks held on 29th-30th September, 1938 which led to the signing of the Munich Agreement.

Hitler goes to war, 1939

During 1939 Hitler strengthened earlier agreements with Italy and signed a non-aggression pact with Russia. This contained secret clauses for the two countries to divide up Poland. At the beginning of September German troops invaded Poland and wiped out the hated "Danzig corridor". This time Britain and France took action and declared war. There were a few months of "phoney war" in the West with little significant action. Then, in the spring of 1940, Hitler invaded Scandinavia, Holland and Belgium. The Germans pressed on westwards into France, pushing back and outflanking the Allied armies. British troops were rescued

German troops pulling down a border barrier bearing the Polish eagle, at the time of the invasion of Poland.

from the beaches of Dunkirk by a flotilla of ships, large and small. On 13th June, Paris fell. Meanwhile, Mussolini had invaded North Africa. Over the following year, German troops invaded Yugoslavia, Greece and Crete, and in the spring of 1941 Hitler made the crucial decision to invade Russia, intending to occupy her as far as the Ural mountains and to drive the Russians back into Siberia.

During the summer of 1941 German troops advanced hundreds of miles. Up to this point, Hitler had been amazingly successful. But when he ordered an attack on Moscow before winter, a very wet autumn followed by a severe, early winter caused havoc in the German Army. The soldiers were short of warm clothing. Even the petrol froze. Russian troops vanished into the forests to conduct guerilla warfare and the Germans were forced to retreat seventy miles. Hitler promptly sacked the generals concerned. In mid-1942 he decided to concentrate his forces further south. He reduced Stalingrad to rubble with bombs and shells, but the Russians counter-attacked. 93,000 Germans were forced to surrender in January 1943. Further defeats followed as the Germans fell back.

By now, Hitler also had problems elsewhere. Following the Japanese attack in December 1941 on Pearl Harbor, the American naval base in the Hawaiian islands in the Pacific, Hitler declared war on the U.S.A., perhaps hoping that the Japanese would join the war against Russia. But they did not do so. Hitler was now fighting three major world powers – Britain, America and Russia. The first front to collapse was North Africa. Hitler had sent Rommel there to help the Italians, who were in trouble, but the "Desert War" was lost after Montgomery's victory at El Alamein. In May 1943, after a bloody campaign in Tunisia, the last Axis troops were forced out of North Africa. Shortly afterwards Allied troops crossed over to Sicily and Italy. Mussolini was quickly over-thrown and Italy surrendered, but the Germans occupied the northern part of the peninsula and stemmed the Allied advance. However, the Germans continued their retreat in Eastern Europe, and in June 1944 Allied troops landed in

In September 1944 57,000 German prisoners-of-war were paraded through Moscow. It was thought inappropriate for them to be seen in Red Square so they were instead marched along the Lenin Highway.

France on D-Day. Hitler now faced a desperate war on three fronts (Italian, French and Russian) as the Allies bombed German cities relentlessly.

The strain takes its toll, 1942-4

Hitler's response to these setbacks was to isolate himself more and more from reality. In the years before 1939 he spoke regularly in public at rallies and on other occasions. He made only seven major speeches in 1941. By March 1942 Goebbels was shocked to notice how the Russian invasion had affected Hitler's health. "He has become quite grey – merely talking about the cares of the winter makes him seem to have aged very much." He suffered from giddiness and hated the sight of snow. He was less prepared than ever to listen to advice and was so furious over the 1942 defeats in Russia that he refused even to eat with his staff officers. He lived increasingly underground at Rastenburg, relying on the pills and medicines prescribed by his doctor, Theodor Morell, a man of very doubtful medical ability. He insisted on having his food tasted for him in case it had been poisoned; he relied increasingly on astrological messages from the stars, and he seemed even to be suffering from the delusion that dividing an army unit in half doubled the total number of soldiers at his command.

By July 1944 the plotters knew that Germany was facing total defeat. This would be a defeat much more devastating even than in 1918. Then, Germany had not been occupied or even invaded; the surrender took place in France. This time, many major German cities would be reduced to rubble. The Russians would march in from the East – Communists bent on revenge – while American, British and French troops advanced from the West. Germany might even cease to exist. And Germany's collapse was being supervised by a ruler who was now clearly incapable of making sensible decisions or of listening to discussion. Urgent and drastic action was needed to avert the terrible prospect which now confronted them; it might already be too late to persuade the Allies to make peace, but it was at least worth a chance. Some of the conspirators were also devout Christians (notably the members of the Kreisau Circle, see page 55), men who believed that they and their fellow Germans had cooperated with Hitler's evil deeds for too long. If they succeeded in killing him, they would at least partly make up for that co-operation. If they failed and had to suffer as a result, their suffering would be an act of penitence for not opposing Hitler earlier. Either way, that bomb had got to be planted.

Army resistance: Why was it so late and ineffective?

The July Plot was the only major show of German resistance to Hitler between his rise to power in 1933 and his death in 1945. There was never any mass revolt against him by German civilians. The plot was undertaken by comparatively few men and they were all either Army officers or leading figures in politics and other fields. It was a revolt by the ruling class, carried out by the only group which had the potential strength to resist Hitler successfully – the Army. No-one else had the training or equipment to match the S.S.

But the revolt took a very long time to come. By July 1944 Hitler had been in power for eleven years. The generals have received a great deal of criticism for their weak and belated resistance and it is important to understand why it took so long for the opposition to act.

For three hundred years army officers had enjoyed a highly respected and privileged position in Germany. Many of them were *Junkers* – aristocratic landowners with large estates. Their families had served the German monarchy as soldiers and government officials for generations. They had reluctantly accepted that the monarchy had to disappear after the defeat of 1918. However, they had no love for the republic which came into being after that and which lasted until Hitler came to power in 1933. They disliked its liberal constitution – one of the most democratic which Europe had ever seen – and its politicians, many of whom were socialists who were openly hostile to both kings and professional soldiers. Some officers secretly backed plans to overthrow it.

After 1918 official army policy was to remain "above" day-to-day political arguments. Even so, some generals did involve themselves in politics in the late 1920s, and made it difficult for any government to win enough popular support to cope with Hitler. The one general who wanted to stand up to Hitler, Interior Minister Wilhelm Groener, was forced to resign in 1932 when he tried to crack down on the street violence of the Nazi stormtroopers. Chancellor Brüning was forced to resign partly because of opposition from the Army. And later in the year Chancellor Franz von Papen was removed from office partly because General Schleicher convinced President Hindenburg that his unpopular policies would lead to a general strike which would leave Germany defenceless against an invasion by either Russia or France. When Hitler became Chancellor in 1933, the Army adopted a "wait and see" position, reassured by the fact that General Blomberg had a cabinet seat as War Minister, while the anti-Nazi General Hammerstein was Chief of the General Staff. He openly doubted Hitler's suitability as a leader in talks with Field Marshal von Hindenburg, the aged President.

President Hindenburg with Hitler. Once Hindenburg had been persuaded to make Hitler Chancellor, he quickly became too elderly to prevent the reign of terror which followed.

Hitler woos the generals, 1933-7

Many military leaders naturally liked the prospect of rearmament, which would give them more men and new equipment. But Hitler recognized that the Army had the power to overthrow him. He was keen to win its support, and he made sure that one of his first engagements as Chancellor, three days after his appointment, was a meeting with top military leaders, to reassure them about his plans. He also pleased officers by ending the power of civilian courts over them and by doing away with the system introduced by the Republican politicians of the 1918-33 period whereby ordinary soldiers were allowed to elect representatives to campaign for their interests in meetings with senior officers. In March 1933 he went with senior military figures to a ceremony in the Garrison Church at Potsdam, the burial place of Germany's military heroes. It was a deliberate bid to win army support.

Nonetheless, by 1934 the Army was deeply worried about the street violence of Röhm and his S.A. stormtroopers. Officers saw the fat, vulgar ex-sergeant-major as a power-crazed thug. But Röhm wanted the S.A. and the Army to be combined, with himself as Defence Minister. Army leaders were appalled; Hitler feared resistance. On 11th April he secretly met army and navy chiefs on a cruiser in the Baltic Sea and made a deal. The Army would continue to be the only official military organization in Germany; the S.A. would be suppressed – although army leaders did not know the bloodbath he was planning. In return, the Army would back Hitler as President when the aged Hindenburg died.

On 30th June the S.A. was wiped out in the "Night of the Long Knives". Five weeks later Hindenburg died and Hitler became Head of State and Commander-in-Chief of the Armed Forces. He persuaded the forces to swear an oath of loyalty to him. Although two ex-generals who had opposed Hitler were murdered in the June purge, the Army offered no resistance; the generals were pleased to see the end of the S.A. and did not yet appreciate the dangerously rapid rise of the S.S. They must not break their oath; breaking promises was not the behaviour of officers and gentlemen. Blomberg and Fritsch (Hammerstein's successor) were weak men, no match for Hitler. Only Admiral Canaris and General Oster in the *Abwehr* – Hitler's counter-intelligence – were active plotters from an early stage.

Hitler falls out with the generals, 1938   As well as welcoming rearmament, many officers backed attempts to break the Versailles treaty. But compulsory military service brought a new type of officer into the Army, not necessarily a gentleman and often a dedicated Nazi, trained in the Hitler Youth. Some generals, notably Beck –

Admiral Wilhelm Canaris, German Chief of Intelligence, later executed on Hitler's orders. Although he was always against any attempt to assassinate Hitler, he was a leading figure in the Resistance and was arrested and executed after the July Plot.

who played such a leading role in the July Plot – believed that Germany needed to expand but that the speed of Hitler's policies was very dangerous. Germany was unprepared for war, and Britain and France would fight.

In 1938, after his successes over the Rhineland and Austria, Hitler decided to get rid of Blomberg and Fritsch. Blomberg was accused of disgracing the Army by marrying a prostitute, Fritsch of being a homosexual. The evidence against Fritsch was totally false but, feeling that the 1934 oath must be honoured, he merely observed, "This man is Germany's destiny and this destiny will run its course to the end," and resigned. Hitler then retired sixteen other senior generals whom he regarded as incompetent or defeatist; forty-four others were transferred to new posts. Loyal Nazis replaced those who retired. Beck's warnings about Hitler's dangerous foreign policy seemed to be proved wrong by Hitler's dramatic success in extracting concessions from Neville Chamberlain at Munich.

The generals and the war

When war came in 1939, army leaders gave it their patriotic support. Oster's group did try to kill Hitler later that year. There was also an explosion in the Munich Beer Hall where Hitler had tried to seize power in 1923, shortly after he visited it for an anniversary celebration. The "Zossen" conspiracy – a plan for Hammerstein to organize Hitler's arrest in Poland – failed when Hitler changed his travel plans at a late stage.

While General von Tresckow tried to organize a bomb to kill Hitler in 1943, Beck was attempting to persuade generals on the Russian front to revolt after the Stalingrad defeat. He was unsuccessful, and his attempts were ended by a cancer operation shortly afterwards. There were at least three other attempts to kill Hitler that year, usually by explosives hidden in overcoats. An air raid prevented Tresckow's officers trying again in January 1944. As we saw on pages 8-9, Stauffenberg made two attempts in July before the 20th.

The Army has often been criticized for giving Hitler too little opposition, too late. Its critics emphasize the planning mistakes in the July Plot itself, especially the failure to win control of the radio stations and of Rastenburg's communications system. Some say that the plot took place only when the generals, bitter after Hitler blamed them for D-Day, felt that their last chance had come – the S.S. had recently arrested large numbers of resistance members. Some say that the plot was nothing more than an attempt to avoid total defeat.

Maybe the Army felt bound by its oath. Maybe officers felt they should keep out of politics. Maybe they feared that a revolt would cause civil war. But they faced huge difficulties in an S.S.-dominated state. Even so, it is hard to avoid the feeling that the army leaders were weak and hesitant. As Captain Hermann Kaiser, one of Fromm's officers, observed, "One wants to act when he receives orders, and the other to give the orders when the action starts." No-one, it seems, dared actually to make the decisive move – except Stauffenberg.

Which other groups in Germany resisted Hitler?

The opposition and the S.S.

The fact that the July Plot was carried out by the Army does not mean that this was the only source of resistance to Hitler. Many of the plotters had close links with men in other walks of life. We shall never know the precise identity or numbers of Hitler's active opponents; the S.S. naturally did not wish to publicize any large-scale opposition, and opponents obviously would not willingly identify themselves for fear of arrest. While it is clear that many Germans preferred to turn a blind eye to Hitler's activities, a significant number did not do so.

The other political parties

Within a year of coming to power, Hitler crushed all the rival political parties and absorbed the Trades Unions into his own Nazi labour organization, the D.A.F. (*Deutsche Arbeitsfront*). The group which might have been expected to oppose him most actively was the Communists (K.P.D.). But their leadership was weak – and this explains their very poor election performance compared with Hitler's in 1929-33, a period of high unemployment when they might have been expected to capture wide support. The Nazis blamed them for the Reichstag (Parliament building) fire very successfully in February 1933, and the S.S. paid special attention to them from then on. Apart from encouraging some sabotage in factories and distributing illegal pamphlets, they were able to do little. They underestimated Hitler, expecting him to hold power for a very short time before the "second stage" of revolution took place, as in Russia in 1917, with the workers seizing power. Stalin, the Russian Communist dictator, who might have given them active support, preferred to do nothing, hoping that Hitler would cause chaos and, eventually, civil war from which the Communists would be able to seize power themselves. The last significant Communist group in Germany was smashed early in 1944.

The Socialists (S.P.D.) were the largest political party in Germany in the years immediately after the First World War and had been the one which most underestimated Hitler – although they were the only party brave enough to oppose his Enabling Bill banning all other parties. They, too, found that the S.S. made active large-scale resistance impossible, and they lost their main power base when Hitler took over the

Trades Unions. Until the early 1940s, there was little hope of any cooperation between them and the Communists. The S.P.D. believed that a system of parliamentary elections had positive virtues, while the K.P.D. despised such elections as a compromise of revolutionary principles. But one Socialist leader, Wilhelm Leuschner, did succeed in making links with the Army, through General Hammerstein, and with some Conservative politicians.

There was also opposition to Hitler from an élite group of Conservatives. These included General Beck himself, Johannes Popitz (who had been Prussian Finance Minister), Ulrich von Hassell (German Ambassador in Rome until

Ulrich von Hassell (former German Ambassador to Rome) on trial. He was highly respected by all the other conspirators and played a major role in keeping the German Resistance in touch with sympathizers abroad.

Hitler sacked him in 1938) and Carl Gördeler (Lord Mayor of Leipzig from 1930-37). Gördeler in particular was a tireless organizer, constantly travelling to try to unite the various opposition groups. But this group has been criticized by many historians as having too many ideas about the sort of Germany which ought to come about after Hitler, while making no actual moves to get rid of him. Many of them

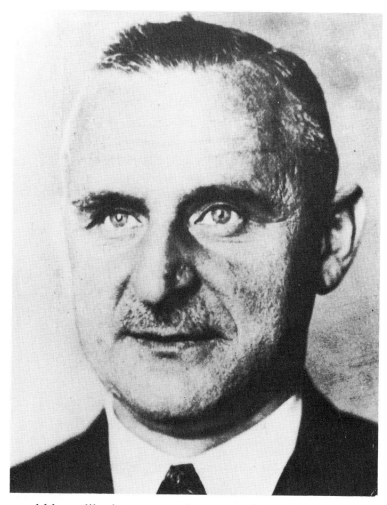

Carl Friedrich Gördeler, Mayor of Leipzig, 1930-7. A tireless organizer, he was seen by many Germans opposed to Hitler as a future Chancellor once Hitler had been removed.

would have liked to restore the monarchy and they believed that government by the nobility, rather than a new democratic republic on 1918-33 lines, was what was needed. They seemed unable to accept that the Allies would insist on total victory and that, for a time at least, Germany would not be a major European power. Nevertheless, they were a brave and well-intentioned group.

Religious opposition to Hitler

The Kreisau Circle, with whom the Conservatives had a number of links, was an interesting contrast to them. This small group of officers and civilians, who thought that Hitler had been a catastrophe, believed that Germany after Hitler would have to be "rechristianized". They included Count Helmuth von Moltke (a descendant of a famous German Field Marshal) and a well-known philosopher and Oxford scholar, Adam von Trott zu Solz. This group was much less anti-Communist than the Conservatives, and more realistic about Germany's immediate future. But it, too, spent more time talking about ideals for the future than about how to remove Hitler immediately.

The Churches were another focus of opposition. The Roman Catholic Centre Party had made an agreement with Hitler in 1933 by which it would not oppose him politically if Catholic schools were protected. There has been a great deal of argument amongst historians about whether the Catholic Church and its Popes should have resisted Hitler more

Dietrich Bonhöffer. A leading figure in the Church resistance to Hitler, he became a double-agent in Canaris's counter-espionage service and maintained many links with supporters abroad. He is regarded as one of the great religious thinkers of the twentieth century.

actively, but there were certainly many brave Catholic leaders who did so. Cardinal Faulhaber of Munich preached a series of sermons about the idea of Justice in the Old Testament – coded attacks on the injustice of Hitler's government. Two other Cardinals spoke out directly against Hitler's programme to exterminate the old and the handicapped. Only their great local popularity saved them from arrest. Bernhard Lichtenberg called on a congregation in Berlin Cathedral to pray for "Jews and inmates of concentration camps". He was himself to die on the way to one in 1943. A number of Protestant leaders made similar protests, notably Martin Niemöller, who had once supported Hitler but who campaigned actively and successfully against Hitler's attempt to form a Nazi "Reichschurch". It was a leading Protestant theologian, Dietrich Bonhöffer, who dared to preach two dramatic ideas: firstly, that Hitler was the Devil and that resisting and killing him was the duty of every Christian; secondly, that resistance should be seen as an act of penitence – an expression of regret to God – by every German for not opposing Hitler earlier. He was in regular contact with General Oster of the *Abwehr*.

Opposition groups and the Army

There were many other smaller groups, like the White Rose student group executed in 1942-3 for encouraging opposition in the universities. Many army leaders knew many of these brave men and women. But, however brave Hitler's civilian opponents might be, they knew that only the Army had a realistic chance of killing him. It was therefore to the Army that they looked for action. They also looked to the Allies for some encouragement.

Why did the Resistance receive so little help from Allied governments?

The German Resistance and the Allies

On a number of occasions the German Resistance made contact with the Allies. Gördeler visited London in 1937 and 1939. Schlabrendorff, one of Tresckow's officers, met Churchill in London in 1939. Bonhöffer met George Bell, Bishop of Chichester and one of the Resistance's closest British contacts, in Sweden in 1942. Gördeler met a number of Allied diplomats there a year later. Adam Trott visited England and America in 1939, but found Chamberlain's response "icy". The head of American Intelligence in Europe, Allen Dulles, arrived in Switzerland in November 1942 and established close contact with a number of the army plotters through Hans Gisevius, the German Vice-Consul in Zürich. He sent regular reports back to Washington.

Nevertheless, the Allied response was never more than lukewarm. One American historian summed up Dulles' efforts in a single question: "In which Washington waste-paper basket did these reports end their existence?" Dulles and the Germans were both naturally disappointed by this response.

Why were the Allies so cautious?

It is easy to be critical of Allied governments for this, but they were in a difficult position. The S.S. was skilful at planting agents and double agents; could the Allies be sure that they could trust the Resistance leaders? The information they received was inevitably rather sketchy and incomplete; could they be sure that they had an accurate picture of the situation? What were the true motives of men like Gördeler – a genuine desire to smash the evil of Hitler and to save humanity and human lives, or merely a desire to help Germany avoid total defeat? Whereas Resistance leaders in other countries were, without doubt, patriots fighting the German invader, the German Resistance could be seen as actually unpatriotic and therefore suspect.

There were other good reasons for the Allied attitude. The alliance after 1941 between England, America and Russia was a fragile one. But it was essential to maintain it if Hitler was to be defeated, and separate talks between one of these countries and any German group might endanger it. At the Casablanca Conference of 1943, Allied leaders therefore decided to accept nothing less than Germany's total surrender, even if this meant a wholesale invasion and occupation. No-one was prepared to risk giving another rabble-rouser the chance to claim that Germany had not really been defeated, but that she had been "stabbed in the back" by traitors – as Hitler had claimed after the Armistice of 1918.

While Churchill and, to a lesser extent, President Roosevelt of the U.S.A. were always suspicious of their Russian ally, Josef Stalin, they could not foresee that the total defeat of Germany would result in the establishment of Russian control over large areas of Eastern Europe. If they had known this, perhaps their response to Gördeler and his friends might have been more sympathetic.

Public opinion and the Allied governments

Finally, there was a feeling that ordinary people at home, especially in Britain, might not accept any compromise with Germans, even if Hitler were killed. Allied propaganda had repeatedly stressed that all Germans should be treated as Hitler's followers – something which had been necessary to ensure that the war effort received full support at home. Some British had supported Chamberlain's attempts to satisfy Hitler up to the Munich Conference in 1938, but almost no-one believed afterwards that Chamberlain had been right. It would be very hard suddenly to try to explain to the British people now that talks would take place with "good" Germans.

Conclusion

In the end, therefore, Churchill and his fellow leaders decided to ignore the pleas of Bishop Bell and Allen Dulles and to give little or no encouragement to the German Resistance. Offering crumbs of hope to the plotters might have encouraged the German Army to revolt earlier against Hitler, but it would have been a policy full of huge risks. The Allied policy was almost certainly right. But we cannot be sure how events would have turned out in Germany if the plotters had been given more support.

The reckoning: Was the plot a pointless one?

Hitler's revenge When Hitler broadcast to the Germans on the evening of 20th July, he promised revenge. Over the next few months that revenge was truly terrifying. Police records list 7,000 arrests; as many as 5,000 people may have been executed. Many of the victims were dragged before the "People's Court" to be insulted and screamed at by its President, Roland Freisler. Most had already been tortured.

They were forced to appear in shabby clothes, without belts to prevent their trousers falling down. They were not allowed their false teeth. Defence lawyers did little to help them; some actually added accusations to those of the prosecution. Only a direct hit on the court-house in February 1945 by an American bomb which killed Freisler brought the grisly farce to an end.

Some victims were hanged slowly by piano wire from meathooks borrowed from slaughterhouses. The trials and executions were carefully filmed. Hitler watched them unmoved; Goebbels is said nearly to have fainted when he saw them. The films were shown to soldiers as a warning, but many walked out, a brave gesture of disgust. The films were probably destroyed on Hitler's orders shortly before he died. Relatives of the accused, and anyone who had sheltered them, were sent to concentration camps. Many died there in the final months of the war.

Others avoided the court, but did not escape Hitler's anger. Twelve hours after the collapse of the plot General von Tresckow, the leading conspirator on the Russian front, blew himself to pieces with a hand grenade. Two field marshals and one general committed suicide in France. The Germans' greatest war hero, Erwin Rommel, was named as a conspirator by another officer who was being tortured. He was at home, recovering from severe injuries, on 14th October when the S.S. surrounded his house. He was given a choice: arrest and disgrace or suicide and a hero's state funeral with the promise of no action against his relatives. He took poison in an S.S. car on a country road soon afterwards. The hospital told his wife that he had had a brain seizure caused by his war injuries, and Hitler made his funeral a major propaganda occasion; he dared not admit publicly that Rommel had deserted him. Meanwhile in Paris, General

Stülpnagel had received the dreaded summons to Berlin. His guards let him stop on the way; there was a shot. Stülpnagel was found struggling in a canal, one eye shot away. The other one had to be removed; he had to be carried to both his trial and execution.

The end of the war – and of Hitler

A Russian soldier in the Reich Chancellery bunker. He is sitting on the sofa on which Hitler is reported to have killed himself.

Nine months after the July Plot, the inevitable defeat came. Allied troops raced towards Berlin from both the West and the East. Hitler shot himself in his underground bunker. His last insult to the Army which he believed had betrayed him both in the plot and on the battlefields was to appoint the Navy chief, Admiral Dönitz, as his successor. A week later, on 7th May, Germany surrendered.

Lest we forget Nearly all the plotters were dead. Theologian Dietrich Bonhöffer was one of the last to die, executed by the S.S. just two weeks earlier. They had made many mistakes in the way they carried out their plot. Many were much too hesitant in their resistance, although the difficulties they had faced were huge. Some, no doubt, hoped merely to save Germany from total defeat. Others were genuinely keen to make up for the crimes Hitler had committed against humanity, for the fact that the Germans had let him carry them out by not opposing him at the start, and for turning a blind eye when the concentration camps opened in 1933. But it is important to remember the bravery of the German Resistance and the fact that there were Germans who were ready to stand up against Hitler and his evil. None more so than Claus von Stauffenberg.

Further reading

THE EVENTS

The July Plot
Roger Maxwell & Heinrich Fraenkel, *The July Plot*, The Bodley Head, 1964.

THE INVESTIGATION

The German Army
Sir John Wheeler Bennett, *The Nemesis of Power*, Macmillan, 1953
Gordon Craig, *The Politics of the Prussian Army 1640-1945*, O.U.P, 1955
Albert Seaton, *The German Army 1933-45*, Weidenfeld & Nicolson, 1982

The German Resistance
Hermann Graml and others, *The German Resistance to Hitler*, Batsford, 1970
Hans Rothfels, *The German Opposition to Hitler*, Oswald Wolff, 1961

General Accounts of Nazism
Karl Dietrich Bracher, *The German Dictatorship*, Peregrine, 1978
Alan Bullock, *Hitler: A Study in Tyranny*, Pelican, 1962
William Shirer, *The Rise & Fall of the Third Reich*, Pan 1964
Norman Stone, *Hitler*, Coronet, 1982

For Reference on Individuals
Joachim C. Fest, *The Face of the Third Reich*, Penguin, 1979
Louis L. Snyder, *Encyclopaedia of the Third Reich*, Robert Hale, 1976
Robert Wistrich, *Who's Who in Nazi Germany*, Weidenfeld & Nicolson, 1982

Documents
Jeremy Noakes and Geoffrey Pridham, *Documents on Nazism 1919-45*, Jonathan Cape, 1974

Illustrated Histories
John Bradley, *The Illustrated History of the Third Reich*, Bison Books, 1978
Ed. Herbert Walther, *Hitler*, Bison Books, 1978

Index